W9-AZM-037

This book belongs to

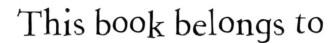

Written by Sue Nicholson
Illustrated by Capucine Mazille

First published by Parragon in 2008

Parragon
Queen Street House
4 Queen Street
Bath BA1 1HE, UK

Please retain information for future reference.

Copyright © Parragon Books Ltd 2008

All rights reserved. No part of this publication may be reproduced, stored in a retrieval system or transmitted, in any form or by any means, electronic, mechanical, photocopying, recording or otherwise, without the prior permission of the copyright holder.

ISBN 978-1-4075-2166-4

Printed in China

My tooth is loose!

PaRragon

Bath · New York · Singapore · Hong Kong · Cologne · Delhi · Melbourne

When Daniel woke up one Saturday morning, one of his teeth felt strange. He pushed it with his tongue. It moved! He pressed it with his finger. It was definitely loose!

Daniel leaped out of bed and raced down to the kitchen to tell Ryan, his big brother.

"My tooth is wonky!" he cried.

Ryan smiled. "Don't look so shocked, Dan," he said. "Everyone's teeth start to get loose when they're about your age —and you're six, right?"
Daniel nodded.

"You've got milk teeth, you see, not real grown-up teeth like mine," Ryan explained. "Your grown-up teeth start growing and push your milk teeth out."

"Push them out?" said Daniel. "How will I eat?"

Ryan laughed. "They won't all fall out at the same time! And every time you lose one, the tooth fairy will visit you in the night!"

"Tooth fairy?" cried Daniel. "I don't believe in fairies!"

"Really," said Ryan. "Well I bet you'll believe in this one because she'll swap your tooth for a shiny coin!"

"Hmmm," said Daniel. "But how does the tooth fairy know when you've lost a tooth?" he asked.

"It's magic!" replied Ryan, winking. "You put your tooth in a little tin under your pillow before you go to sleep. In the morning, the tooth has vanished and the tooth fairy has left you a coin—maybe even two coins if your tooth is especially clean and shiny!"

"That's AMAZING!" shouted Daniel. "How many milk teeth do I have?"

"About twenty," replied Ryan.

"WOW!" cried
Daniel as he imagined
what he could buy.

"I could buy a ball . . .

a racing car . . .

an electric train . . .

or, best of all, a pirate's costume!"

"Hold on," laughed Ryan. "You might not lose all your milk teeth until you're about twelve. You'll have to be patient and save up!"

"Well, I could start with a pirate eye patch!" said Daniel. "Jake's coming to stay next weekend, and we're going to play pirates. I could buy a pirate eye patch and be One-eyed Dan! Do pirates have loose teeth?"

For the next few days, Daniel wiggled and jiggled his tooth. It did feel a bit looser, but it didn't fall out.

"Do dogs have loose teeth?" he asked Ryan one afternoon when they were taking Fang for a walk.

"Yes, when they're puppies," said Ryan. "Fang's losing his puppy teeth now. He chews things to help his adult teeth come through."

" . . . like my sneakers?" laughed Daniel. "I don't want to chew stinky old shoes to help my tooth come out!"

All the next day, Daniel wiggled and jiggled his loose tooth.
It did feel even looser, but it still didn't fall out.
Feeling fed up, he went to see Ryan, who was
cleaning out his pet hamster, Gnawbert's, cage.

"Do hamsters get loose teeth?" Daniel asked.

"No," replied Ryan. "They have just one set of
teeth that lasts their whole lifetime, but a hamster's
teeth grow all the time.
Gnawbert has to gnaw tough woody things
to keep his teeth clean and stop them from
getting too long."

"Hmmmm," laughed Daniel. "I want my teeth to be clean and strong, but I don't want to gnaw twigs and sticks!"

So Daniel carried on wiggling and jiggling his loose tooth.

He tried pushing it backward and forward . . .

twisting it one way and then the other . . .

. . . he even tried biting and gnawing on tough foods, such as apples and crusty bread. By Friday evening, Daniel felt very fed up.

"It's only two days until Jake comes to stay," he told Ryan, "and my tooth is still just loose. There's no way I'll be able to be One-eyed Dan in our pirate game!"

The next day, Ryan took Daniel to his favorite place for a special treat to cheer him up. They went to the aquarium to look at all the amazing sea life. Daniel liked the sharks best.

"Do sharks lose their teeth?" he asked.

"Yes they do," said Ryan, reading the sign next to the tank. "It says here that some sharks have hundreds of teeth, in rows. If their teeth get broken off when they are hunting and fighting their prey, new ones grow in their place."

"Wow!" said Daniel, pressing his nose to the glass. "But I don't want to feast on fierce fish—even if it does make my teeth fall out!"

"How's your tooth now?" asked Ryan.
Daniel sighed. "It still hasn't fallen out!"
"It won't be long now," said Ryan.
"Stay here. I'll be back in a few minutes."

Ryan went to the aquarium gift store and hunted through the toys and souvenirs. There were fluffy toy octopuses, kites shaped like tropical fish, and all kinds of other fantastic things. But after a few minutes, Ryan found what he was looking for—a small, shiny blue tin.

Ryan went outside to find his brother. They sat down to wait for the dolphin show to begin.

"I've got a present for you, Dan," said Ryan. "You can put your tooth in it when it falls out."

"If it ever falls out!" replied Daniel, laughing. Daniel opened the paper bag and took out the shiny blue tooth tin.

"Wow! that's great!" cried Daniel, jumping up to give Ryan a hug. "Thank you!"

And as Daniel said
"thank you" something amazing
happened! His loose tooth fell out—
well, it flew out—and landed on the ground.

Daniel wasn't sure whether
he believed in the tooth fairy
or not, but he did really want
a pirate's eye patch. So when
he went to bed that night he put
his tin with the tooth inside
under his pillow just in case . . .

and then he fell fast asleep.

The next day, Daniel found two coins—enough to buy a pirate eye patch.

And later that day, One-eyed Daniel and his ship mate Jake set sail.